Government
in Action

Michael Frank

PICTURE CREDITS

Cover (background) ©Vladpans/Panoramic Images, (statue) © Pete Saloutos/CORBIS; Title page, pages 15 (center), 30 (right bottom), 35-a and f © Reuters/CORBIS; pages 2-3, 5 (top) PictureQuest; page 4 © David Butow/CORBIS SABA; page 5 (left bottom) Superstock, (right bottom) © Tiffany M. Hermon/The Image Works; pages 7, 13 (center), 20-21(center), 24 (left top) Bettmann/CORBIS; pages 7 (frame), 32 (bottom) Getty Images; pages 8-9 (sky), 10-11 (sky), 12-13 (sky), 14-15 (sky), 16 (left top), 17 (right middle),18-19 (center bottom), 19 (right top), 21 (right top), 23 (right top), 27 (right top), 31 (right bottom), 34-a, 35-e CORBIS; pages 8 (left middle), 30(right middle), 34-b The Granger Collection, New York; pages 8 (center middle), 26-27 (background) © Joseph Sohm, Visions of America/CORBIS; pages 8 (left middle), 30 (left top) Comstock; pages 8-9 (background) © Galen Rowell/CORBIS; pages 10-11 (background) © William Manning /Corbis; pages 12-13 (background), 25 (left bottom), 34-e © Joe Sohm/The Image Works; pages 16-17 (background) Taxi/Getty Images; page 16 (left bottom) © Larry Lee Photography/CORBIS; pages 17 (right bottom), 30 (right bottom) Brand X Pictures; pages 18 (top), 31 (left bottom and right middle) Photodisc; page 19 (bottom) © Michael Ventura; page 20 © Sitki Tarlan/Panoramic Images; page 21 (right) Hulton Archive/Getty Images; page 23 (right center) © Wally McNamee/CORBIS; pages 25 (right top), 35-d © Tim Carter/PhotoEdit; pages 26 (left), 34-c © Peggy & Ronald Barnett/CORBIS; page 27 (right bottom) detail from *George Washington* by Gilbert Stuart, Museum of the City of New York; page 28 (top) © Alan Schein/CORBIS, (right bottom) © Chris Collins/CORBIS; page 29 (right bottom) © Stock Connection/PictureQuest; page 30 (left middle) © Ed Bock/CORBIS, (right top) © Ariel Skelley/CORBIS; page 32 (bottom) Getty Images; page 33 (left) *The Constitution* by Paul Finkelman, © 2004 National Geographic Society, cover © Getty Images, © Courtesy of the Library of Congress; page 33 (center) *The Spirit of a New Nation* by Kate Connell, © 2002 National Geographic Society, cover © Museum of the City of New York/CORBIS; page 33 (right) *Kids Are Citizens* by Ellen Keller, © 2002 National Geographic Society, cover Linda Bartlett/FOLIO, Inc., Terry Farmer/Stone, Bob Daemmrich Photography, Inc./Pictor, Jean Shapiro Cantu, Marc Pokempner/Stone; page 36 © David Frazier/The Image Works.

Produced through the worldwide resources of the National Geographic Society, John M. Fahey, Jr., President and Chief Executive Officer; Gilbert M. Grosvenor, Chairman of the Board; Nina D. Hoffman, Executive Vice President and President, Books and Education Publishing Group.

PREPARED BY NATIONAL GEOGRAPHIC SCHOOL PUBLISHING

Ericka Markman, Senior Vice President and President, Children's Books and Education Publishing Group; Steve Mico, Senior Vice President, Editorial Director, Publisher; Francis Downey, Executive Editor; Richard Easby, Editorial Manager; Anne Stone, Lori Dibble Collins, Editors; Bea Jackson, Director of Layout and Design; Jim Hiscott, Design Manager; Cynthia Olson, Art Director; Margaret Sidlosky, Illustrations Director; Matt Wascavage, Manager of Publishing Services; Sean Philpotts, Jane Ponton, Production Managers; Ted Tucker, Production Specialist.

MANUFACTURING AND QUALITY CONTROL

Christopher A. Liedel, Chief Financial Officer; Phillip L. Schlosser, Director; Clifton M. Brown III, Manager

◀ **People gather in front of the Capitol in Washington, D.C.**

Contents

Build Background   **4**
What Does Government Do?

1 Understand the Big Idea   **6**
The United States Government

2 Take a Closer Look   **16**
A Visit to Washington, D.C.

3 Make Connections   **24**

Extend Learning   **30**

Glossary   **34**

Index   **36**

CONSULTANT AND REVIEWER
Dr. Peter Hinks, Historian, Wethersfield, Connecticut

BOOK DESIGN/PHOTO RESEARCH
Steve Curtis Design, Inc.

Published by the National Geographic Society
1145 17th Street N.W.
Washington, D.C. 20036-4688

ISBN: 9780792254478

2015
5 6 7 8 9 10 11 12 13 14 15

Printed in Menasha, WI

What Does Government Do?

Government is the group of people who run a country. The government has many jobs.

- It provides services for the people.
- It makes rules that everyone agrees to follow.
- It keeps people safe.

In the United States, people choose their leaders by voting. These leaders make decisions for the people. These leaders run the government.

government – the group of people who run a country

▲ **People vote for people who run the government.**

▲ Government pays for schools to educate people.

▲ Government makes rules that keep things orderly.

▲ Government provides services that keep people safe.

Big Idea
The United States government has three parts.

Set Purpose
Learn what each of the three parts of government does.

The United Gover

In 1787, a group of men decided that the United States needed a new government. They wrote a plan for how this government would work. A plan for a government is called a **constitution**.

The plan they wrote gives the government three jobs:

- To make laws
- To put laws into action
- To make sure that laws are fair

In this book, you will read how the United States government does these jobs.

....
constitution – a plan of government

Questions You Will Explore

How is the United States government set up?

What does government do?

States
nment

▼ American leaders sign the Constitution.

The Three Branches of Government

The United States government has three parts. The parts are the executive, the legislative, and the judicial. The parts are often called branches.

Look at the diagram. It shows the three branches of the United States government. Each branch has its own job. Together, the branches make the government work.

Three Branches of Government

1	2	3

The **legislative branch** makes laws.	The **executive branch** puts laws into action.	The **judicial branch** decides whether laws are fair.

Government Powers

Government needs power to do its job. The United States government is set up so that power is divided among the three branches. No one branch has all the power. Each branch can help control the power of the other two branches. This is called checks and balances.

▼ All three branches of government work in Washington, D.C.

The Legislative Branch

The legislative branch is called Congress. Congress has two parts called the Senate and the House of Representatives. Congress makes the laws that govern the United States.

Each law starts out as a **bill**. A bill is an idea for a new law. A member of Congress writes the bill. Then members of Congress talk about the bill and vote on it. If most of the members of Congress vote for it, the bill is sent to the President.

....
bill – an idea for a law

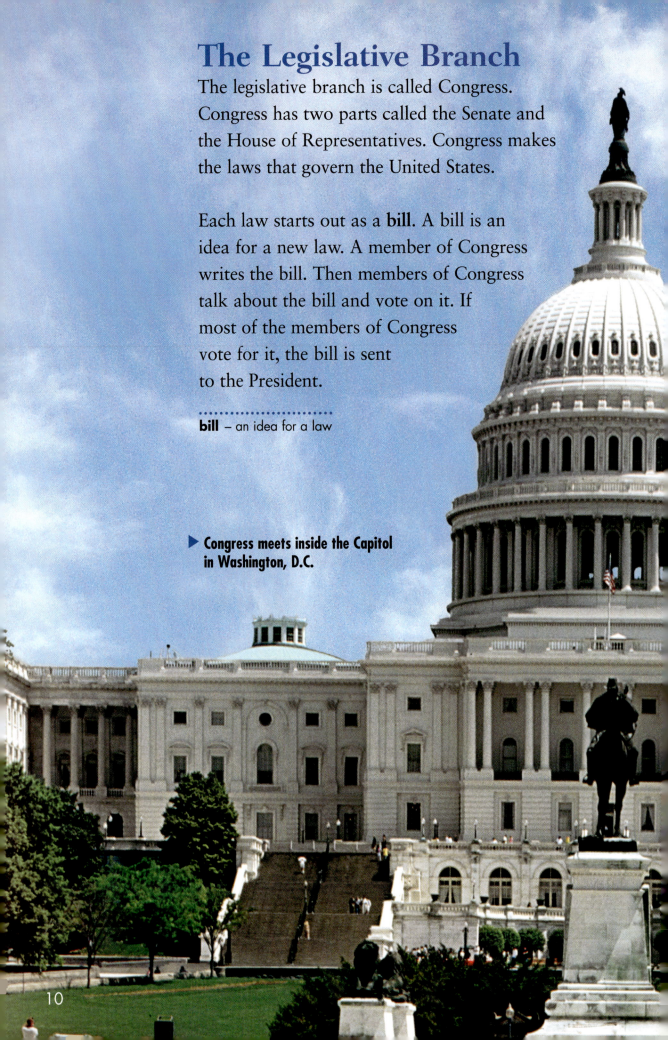

▶ Congress meets inside the Capitol in Washington, D.C.

The Two Parts of Congress

The Senate

- 100 members, called senators. Two senators are elected from each state.

- Senators are elected for six years. They can be reelected.

- Senators must be at least 30 years old.

The House of Representatives

- 435 members, called representatives. Each state has at least one representative. States with the most people have the most representatives.

- Representatives are elected for two years. They can be reelected.

- Representatives must be at least 25 years old.

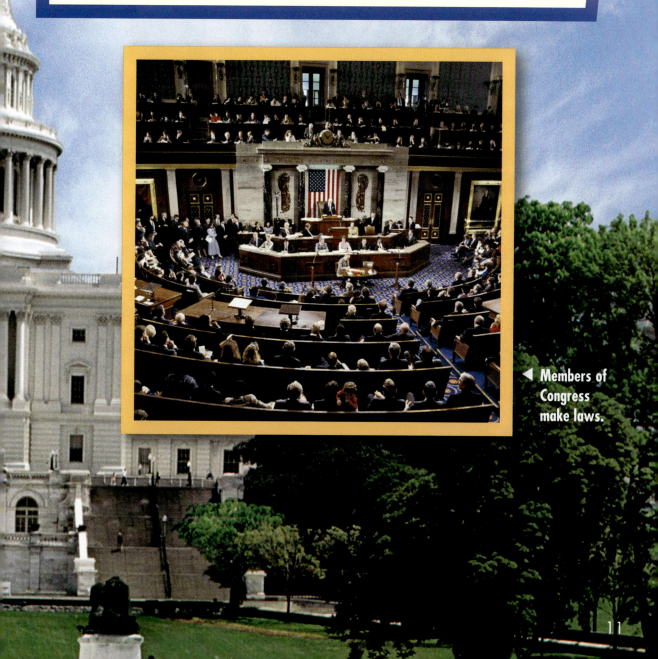

◄ Members of Congress make laws.

The Executive Branch

The President is the leader of the executive branch. The President is also the head of the United States government. The President can do two things with a bill. The President can sign a bill, making it a law. Or the President can **veto** a bill. Veto means to reject.

If the President vetoes a bill, Congress can vote on it again. If two-thirds of the members of Congress vote for the bill, it becomes a law. The President cannot veto it again.

....
veto – to reject

▲ The President lives and works in the White House in Washington, D.C.

The President

- Every United States citizen age 18 and older may vote to determine who will be President.

- The President is elected for four years. He or she may be reelected for another four years.

- The President must be at least 35 years old; have been born a citizen of the United States; and have lived in the United States for at least 14 years.

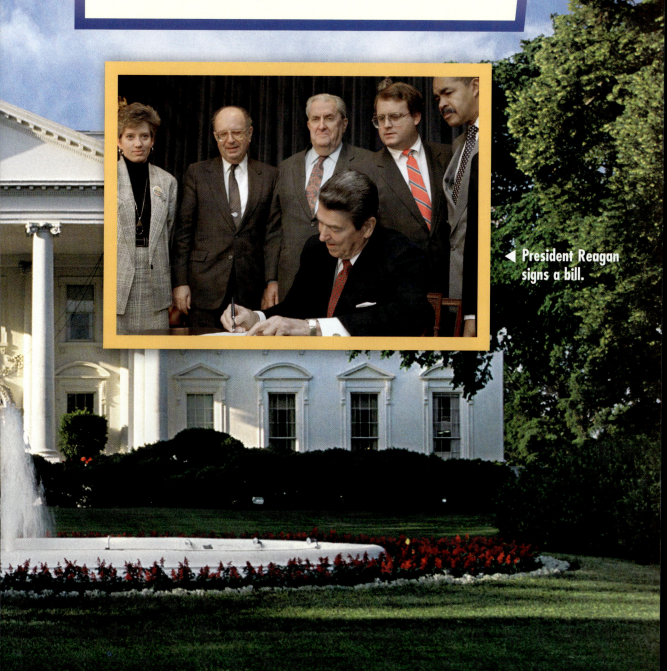

◄ President Reagan signs a bill.

The Judicial Branch

The judicial branch is made up of the Supreme Court and all other **federal** courts. The judicial branch decides whether laws are fair. The Supreme Court is the highest court in the country. It makes the final decision about the fairness of a law. If most of the **justices** say a law is unfair, then it is no longer a law.

federal – part of the United States government

justice – a judge on the Supreme Court

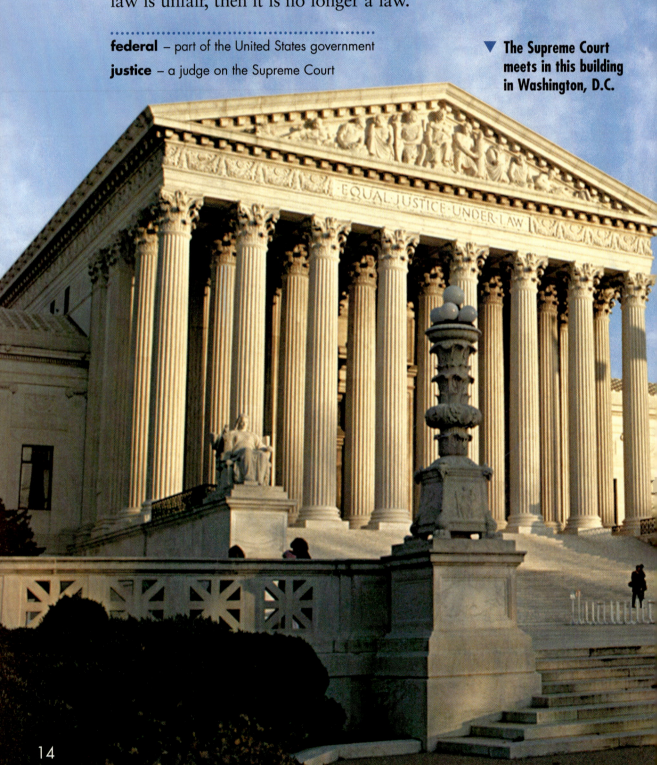

▼ **The Supreme Court meets in this building in Washington, D.C.**

The Supreme Court

- The Supreme Court has nine members.

- The President chooses members of the Supreme Court.

- The Senate must agree with the President's choices. If the Senate does not agree, the President makes another choice.

- Justices serve for life. Justices can retire.

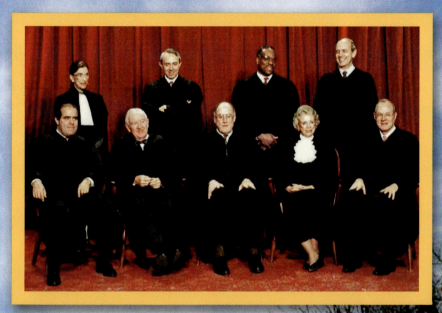

▲ There are nine Supreme Court justices.

Stop and Think!

Why does the United States have three branches of government?

15

A Visit to

Recap
Explain what each of the three branches of government does.

Set Purpose
Read about the city in which the government is located.

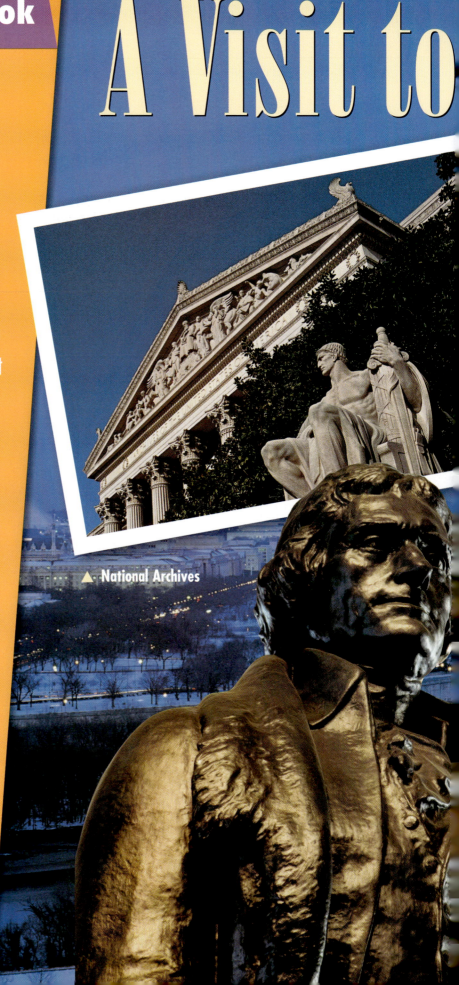

▲ National Archives

Washington, D.C.

My friend Jennifer and I are going to Washington, D.C. We studied government in school this year. We learned about the three branches of government. We also learned about Washington, D.C. This city is home to the federal government.

▼ Jefferson Memorial

◀ Statue of Thomas Jefferson

▲ The National Mall stretches from the
Capitol to the Lincoln Memorial.

Planning Our Trip

There is a lot to see in Washington, D.C.
There are lots of statues and **monuments.**
We are most excited about seeing the National
Archives, the Capitol, the White House, and
the Supreme Court building.

All of these places are located near a large
park. It is called the National Mall. The
mall is two miles long. It runs from the
Capitol to the Lincoln Memorial.

monument – a building that honors a person or an event

The National Archives

Our first stop is the National Archives. An **archive** is a place where important papers are kept. The National Archives houses three of the most important papers in United States history.

The Declaration of Independence was written in 1776. It gives reasons why Americans wanted to form their own country.

We also see the Constitution and the Bill of Rights. The Constitution is the plan for our government. The Bill of Rights tells the rights that all United States citizens have.

archive – a building where important papers are kept

▼ **You can see the Constitution at the National Archives.**

◄ **A statue of Abraham Lincoln sits inside the Lincoln Memorial.**

▲ A huge dome tops the Capitol.

The Capitol Building

Next we go inside the Capitol. That is where Congress meets. It has 550 rooms. We do not have enough time to see all of them. I like the Rotunda best. It is a big, round room in the middle of the building.

There are paintings and statues in the rotunda. We see a statue of Ethan Allen. He was a hero in the American Revolution.

Exploring the Capitol

We also see the two large rooms where the Senate and House of Representatives meet. They are located on either end of the Capitol. Members of Congress meet in these rooms to **debate** and vote on bills.

Each room has a visitor's area. You can sit in these areas and watch the members of Congress. You can hear what they are saying. But you have to be quiet so you do not bother them.

....
debate – to talk about

▶ This statue of Ethan Allen stands in the Rotunda.

▲ Ceremonies are held in the Rotunda.

21

▲ The nine Supreme Court justices sit in these chairs when they hear a case.

The Supreme Court

The Supreme Court is located near the Capitol. A guide shows us the room where the nine justices hear important cases. Each time the justices enter the room, someone says, "Oyez. Oyez." They are French words for "Hear ye. Hear ye," or "Listen up."

The White House

Our last stop is the White House. It is where the President both works and lives.

The President works in the Oval Office. It is a round room. The Oval Office is in part of the building called the West Wing.

Only one President did not work in the White House. He was George Washington. The White House was being built when he was President.

Stop and Think!

What do the buildings in Washington, D.C., have to do with the government?

▲ The President works in the Oval Office.

◄ This statue shows John Marshall. He was a Chief Justice of the Supreme Court.

23

3 **Make**
Connections

Recap
Explain what happens in the White House, the Capitol, and the Supreme Court building.

Set Purpose
Learn more about how the United States government works.

CONNECT WHAT YOU HAVE LEARNED

Government in Action

The United States government has three parts, or branches. Each branch has a different job. Having three branches keeps any one branch from becoming too powerful.

Here are some ideas that you learned about the United States government.

- The Constitution describes how our government works.
- The legislative branch makes the laws.
- The executive branch puts the laws into action.
- The judicial branch decides whether laws are fair.

Check What You Have Learned

What is the job of each branch of government?

24

▲ American leaders sign the Constitution.

▲ Congress meets in the Capitol.

▲ The President works in the White House.

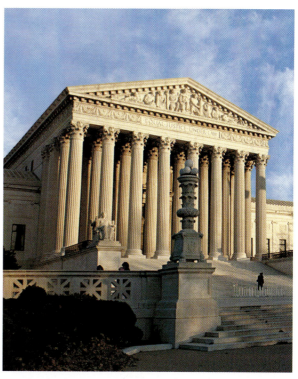

▲ The Supreme Court hears cases in this building.

The First Constitution

▲ The Constitution outlines how our government works.

The Constitution written in 1787 was not the first plan of government for the United States. Six years earlier, the states wrote a plan called the Articles of Confederation.

America's first government was not very powerful. Congress was the only branch of government. It could declare war and make agreements with other countries. But it could not raise taxes. As a result, the government did not have any money.

Some Americans decided that they needed a stronger government. They met in Philadelphia in 1787. They wrote a new Constitution. It is the same one we have today.

What Should the President Be Called?

When Congress first met in 1789, members had lots of decisions to make. John Adams thought "President" did not sound important enough. He wanted the head of the executive branch to be called "His Highness." Many people thought that sounded like something you would call a king. The House of Representatives felt "President" was just fine. The Senate liked something closer to Adams's idea. In the end, the Senate decided to go along with the House.

▲ Americans did not want to be ruled by a king.

▶ George Washington was the first President.

Symbols of Freedom

The American flag and the Great Seal are both symbols of the United States. A symbol is something that stands for something else.

The flag has 13 red and white stripes, plus 50 stars on a blue background. The stripes stand for the original 13 colonies that started our country. There is one star for each state today.

The Great Seal shows an eagle holding an olive branch with arrows in its claws. The olive branch stands for the desire for peace. The arrows show the ability to wage war if necessary.

28

Governments Within a Government

You learned about the federal government. Did you know that each state also has a government? All state governments have three branches. They have legislative, executive, and judicial branches just like the United States government.

◀ **The state capitol of Connecticut**

▲ **The American flag**

▲ **The Great Seal of the United States**

Many kinds of words are used in this book. Here you will learn about words with prefixes. You will also learn about words that sound alike, but have different meanings.

Prefixes

Prefixes are letters added to the beginning of words. A prefix changes the meaning of a word. For example, the prefix *un-* can turn a word into its opposite.

The Supreme Court makes sure laws are **fair.**

Laws should never be **unfair.**

The government makes **important** decisions.

It is **unimportant** which monument we visit first.

Homophones

Homophones are words that sound alike, but have different meanings. Find the homophones below. Then use each word in a sentence of your own.

Their job is to make laws.

There is a book on the table.

All laws should be **fair.**

She paid a **fare** to ride the bus.

The National Mall is **two** miles long.

I am going **to** Washington, D.C.

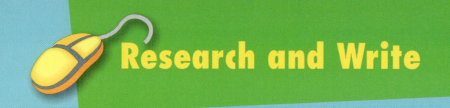

Research and Write

Write About the Government

Choose an issue that is important to you. Research that issue. Then write a letter to your senator or representative about that issue.

Research

Collect books and reference materials, or go online.

Read and Take Notes

As you read, take notes and draw pictures.

Write

Write a letter that explains your ideas concerning the issue that you chose.

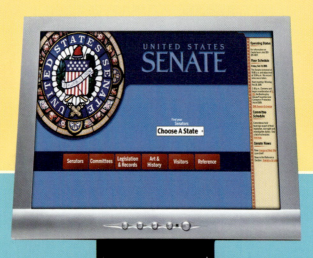

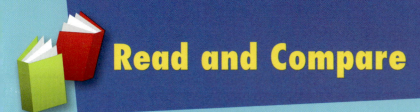

Read and Compare

Read More About Government

Find and read other books about the United States government. As you read, think about these questions.

- What does government do?
- What are the branches of the United States government?
- What does each branch of government do?

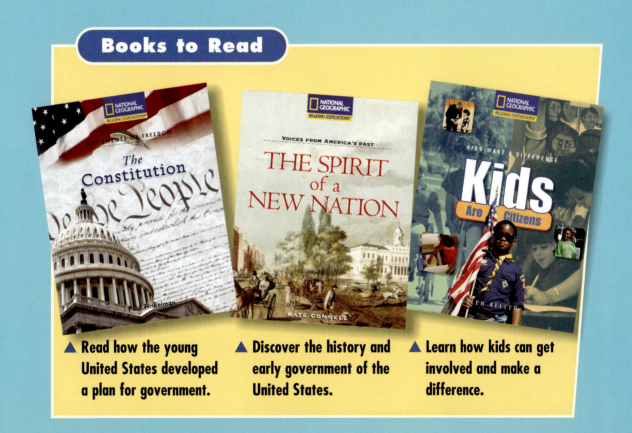

Books to Read

▲ Read how the young United States developed a plan for government.

▲ Discover the history and early government of the United States.

▲ Learn how kids can get involved and make a difference.

Glossary

archive (page 19)
A building where important papers are kept
Our first stop is the National Archives.

bill (page 10)
An idea for a law
Each law starts as a bill.

constitution (page 6)
A plan of government
People wrote the United States Constitution in 1787.

KEY CONCEPT

debate (page 21)
To talk about
Congress meets to debate and vote on bills.

executive branch (page 8)
The government branch that puts laws into action
The head of the executive branch lives and works in the White House.

KEY CONCEPT

federal (page 14)
Part of the United States government
The Supreme Court is one of the federal courts.

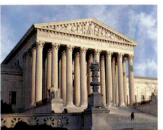

government (page 4)
The group of people who run a country
The government has many jobs.

judicial branch (page 8)
The government branch that decides whether laws are fair
The Supreme Court is part of the judicial branch.

justice (page 14)
A judge on the Supreme Court
The Supreme Court has nine justices.

legislative branch (page 8)
The government branch that makes laws
The legislative branch meets in the Capitol.

monument (page 18)
A building that honors a person or an event
The Lincoln Memorial is a monument in Washington, D.C.

veto (page 12)
To reject
The President can veto a bill.

Index

bill	10, 12, 34
Capitol	3, 10, 18, 20, 21, 22, 25
Congress	10, 11, 12, 20, 21, 25, 26, 27
Constitution	6, 7, 19, 24, 25, 26, 34
Declaration of Independence	19
executive branch	8, 12, 24, 29, 34
federal	14, 17, 29, 34
House of Representatives	10, 11, 21, 27
judicial branch	8, 14, 24, 29, 35
legislative branch	8, 10, 24, 29, 35
National Archives	18, 19, 34
President	12, 13, 23, 25, 27
Senate	10, 11, 21, 27
Supreme Court	14, 15, 18, 22, 23, 25
White House	12, 18, 23, 25